imagine

having asthma

Linda O'Neill

DISCARDED
from
New Hanover County Public Library

NEW HANOVER COUNTY
PUBLIC LIBRARY
201 CHESTNUT STREET
WILMINGTON, NC 28401

The Rourke Press, Inc.
Vero Beach, Florida 32964

©2001 The Rourke Press, Inc.
All rights reserved. No part of this book may be reproduced or utilized
in any form or by any means, electronic or mechanical including photocopying, recording, or
by any information storage and retrieval system without permission in writing from the
publisher.

NOTE: Not all of the children photographed in this book have asthma, but volunteered to be
photographed to help raise public awareness.

PHOTO CREDITS
© Eyewire: cover, page 15; © East Coast Studios: pages 6, 16, 20, 25, 29;
© Timothy L. Vacula: pages 8, 19; © American Academy of Alergy, Asthma and Immunology:
pages 11, 13; © PhotoDisc: page 22

PRODUCED & DESIGNED by East Coast Studios
eastcoaststudios.com

EDITORIAL SERVICES
Pamela Schroeder

Library of Congress Cataloging-in-Publication Data

O'Neill, Linda
    Having asthma / Linda O'Neill.
        p. cm. — (Imagine...)
    Includes index.
    Summary: Discusses the nature, symptoms, triggers, management, and treatment of asthma.
    ISBN 1-57103-379-3
    1. Asthma—Juvenile literature. [1. Asthma. 2. Diseases.] I. Title. II. Imagine (Vero Beach, Fla.)

RC591 .O54 2000
616.2'38—dc21

                                                        00–023921

Printed in the USA

Author's Note

This series of books is meant to enlighten and give children an awareness and sensitivity to those people who might not be just like them. We all have obstacles to overcome and challenges to meet. We need to think of the person first, not the disability. The children I interviewed for this series showed not one bit of self-pity. Their spirit and courage is admirable and inspirational.

Linda O'Neill

Table of Contents

Imagine This

You run to catch up with your friends. Soon you are **wheezing** (WEE zing). You cannot seem to get enough breath. Your chest hurts and your heart is beating very fast. This is what an asthma **flare** (FLAYR), or attack, feels like. It is scary to feel this way. Some people with **asthma** (AZ mah) say it's like trying to breathe air through a straw.

Sometimes running can cause a flare if you have asthma.

What Is Asthma?

Asthma is a breathing problem. At least 12 million people in the United States have asthma. The word asthma means "panting" in Greek. Asthma can start at any age. You don't catch asthma from other people.

Asthma is like having **allergies** (AL er geez). Something, called a **trigger** (TRIG er), makes your airways and lungs react. It gets hard for you to breathe. Asthma is something that doesn't go away. However, there are things you can do to make you feel better.

With asthma, your lungs have a hard time breathing.

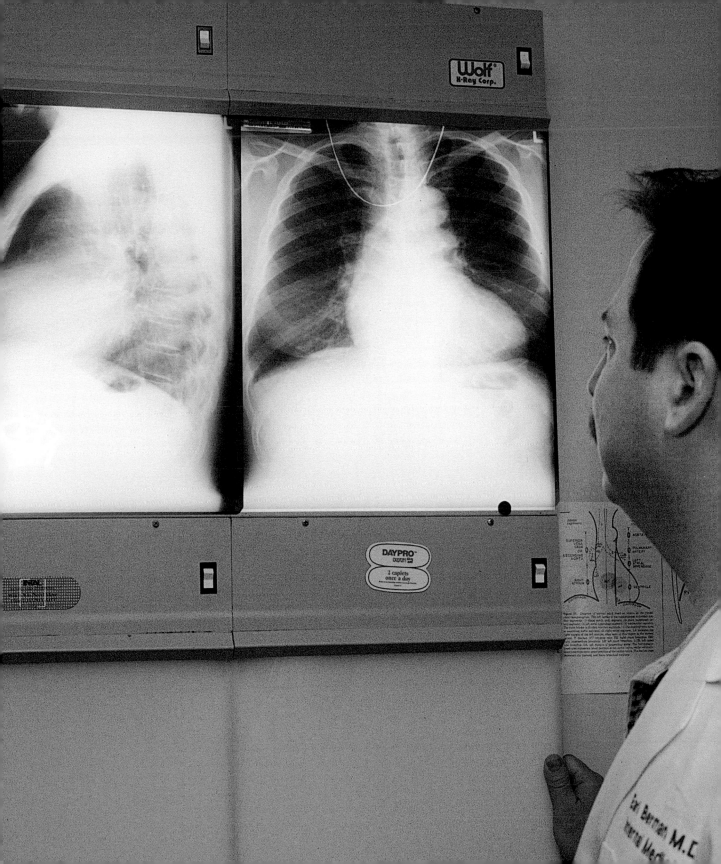

During an asthma flare, the tubes in your lungs swell. The muscles around your air tubes **contract** (con TRAKT) so the airways get even smaller. Your body makes a lot of **mucus** (MYOO cus), like when you have a cold. It is very hard to breathe. People with asthma take medicine during flares to help them breathe. They **inhale** (in HAIL) this medicine to get it into their lungs quickly. This medicine works to open up the air tubes. Once the air tubes are big again, they breathe easier. They take other medicine every day to stop asthma flares from starting.

Taking medicine during a flare opens air tubes to help you breathe easier.

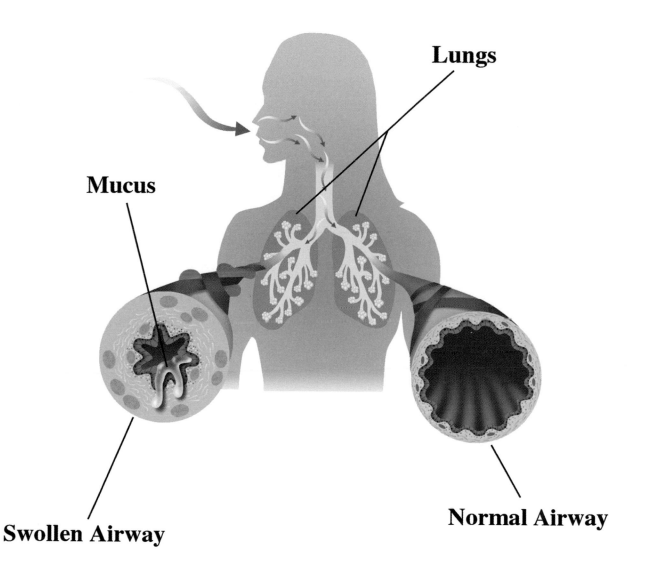

Lungs

Mucus

Swollen Airway

Normal Airway

Know Your Triggers

If you have asthma, it is important to know what your triggers are. A trigger does not cause asthma. A trigger starts an asthma flare. Some of the most common triggers are dog and cat **dander** (DAN der), dust, dust mites, exercise, cold air, and smoke. Some foods can be triggers, too. Almost 80 percent of people with asthma also have allergies. An allergy can trigger an asthma attack.

Some "triggers" are dust, pet dander, and dust mites.

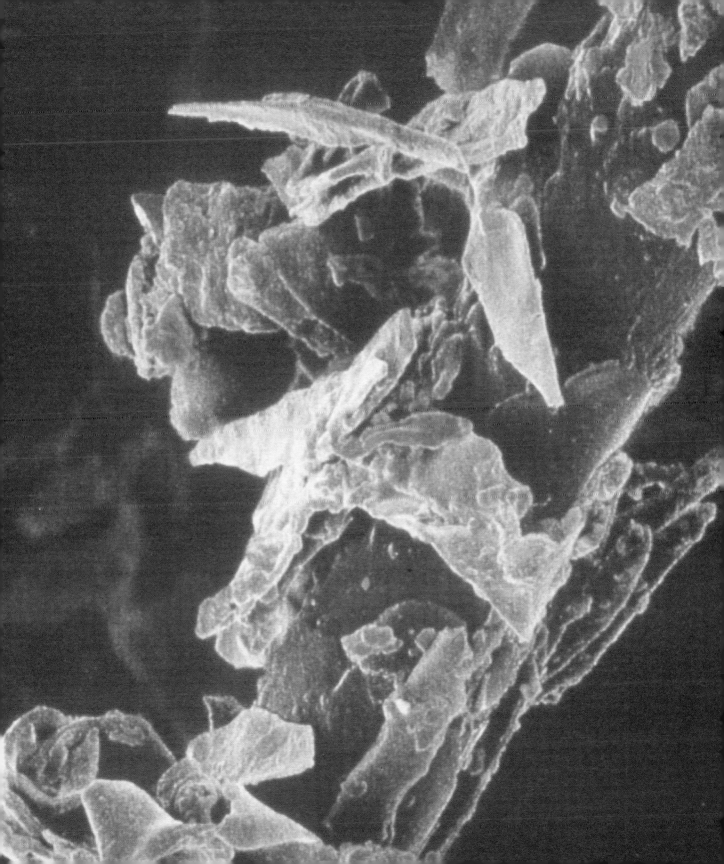

Early Warning Signs

You and your family need to know the early warning signs of an asthma flare. If you know the signs, you can stop an attack by taking your medicine before the flare happens. Some of the signs you need to watch for are:

- You feel tired and your chest feels tight.
- You have a headache.
- You have dark circles under your eyes.
- You can't sleep or have nightmares.
- You are breathing faster than normal.

If you have asthma, a headache can be a warning sign.

Taking Care of Yourself

People with asthma use a peak flow meter. It is a tool that shows how much air you can blow out quickly.

To use a peak flow meter, you take a deep breath. You put the mouthpiece in your mouth. You blow out as hard and fast as you can. The pointer goes up a numbered scale.

The scale uses colors like a traffic light to tell you about your breathing. Green means your breathing is very good. Yellow means you need to be careful. Your breathing is at 50 to 80 percent of what it should be. Red means you need medicine right away.

People with asthma use a peak flow meter to tell them about their breathing.

Treatment

Your **treatment** (TREET ment) may be using an inhaler with a spacer. An inhaler is what you use to take your medicine. The spacer lets more medicine into your lungs. Your school nurse or teacher should know about your asthma. They can help you in case you need your medicine. If you are having a lot of trouble breathing, you may have to go to the hospital for a breathing treatment.

In the hospital, you might use a **nebulizer** (NEB yuh LIE zer). This machine turns your liquid medicine into a mist that you breathe in. You do this for some time until your breathing gets better.

An inhaler gets medicine to your lungs fast.

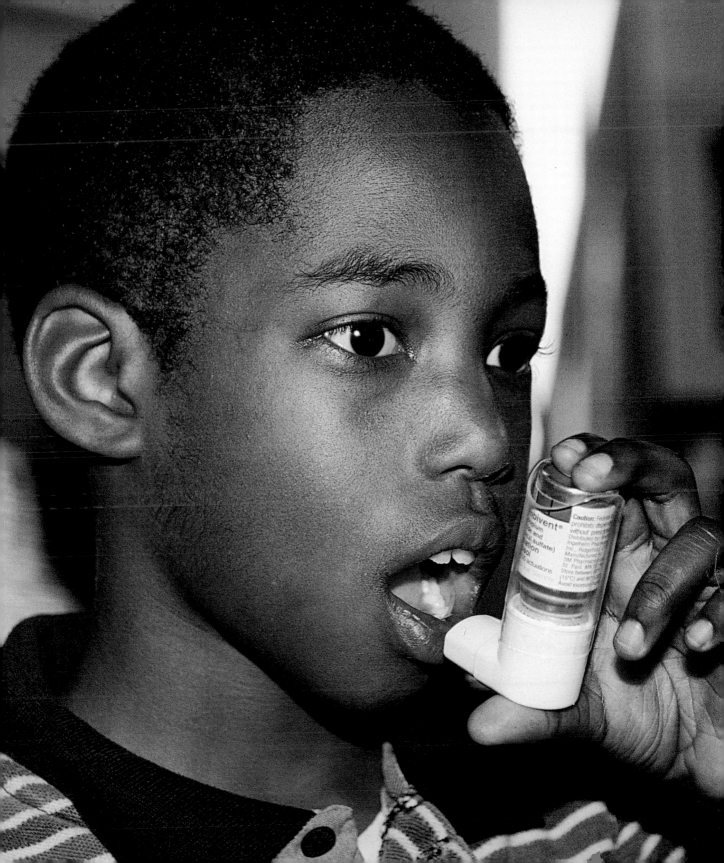

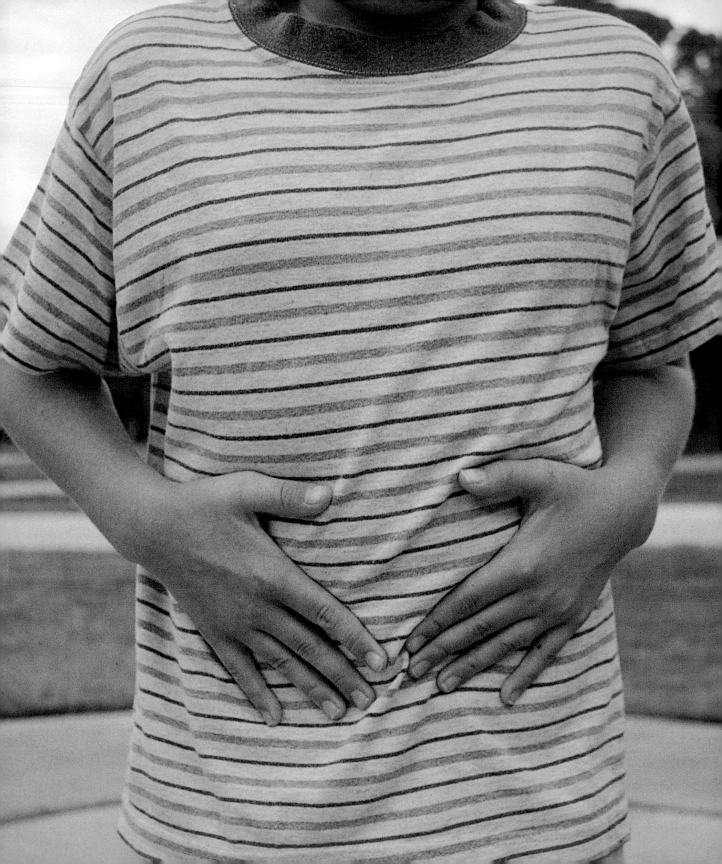

Helping Yourself

There are many things you can do to help your asthma. You can practice breathing exercises. Most people only use the top of their lungs to breathe. Their chests move when they inhale. There is a lot more room for air!

Hold your hand on your tummy. When you breathe in, let the air fill the bottom of your lungs first. Can you feel your tummy moving? Can you feel how much air you are getting? Breathing deeply can help people with asthma.

Practice deep breathing to make your lungs strong.

There are other things you can do to make your lungs stronger. Blowing up balloons is a fun way to exercise your lungs. You can also play a flute or clarinet.

Once you know your triggers, try to stay away from them. Don't go into dusty places if dust is a trigger. Don't own any furry pets if dander is a trigger. Stay away from smoky places. Smoke is not good for anybody's lungs! Ask people not to smoke around you.

Playing the flute is a good exercise for your lungs—and fun, too!

If you get an asthma flare after running or riding your bike, try using your inhaler first. A person with asthma can play any sport if they are careful about taking their medicine. Asthma is about taking care of yourself. Asthma is about thinking ahead and being prepared.

Smoking is not good for anybody's lungs.

Meet Someone Special!

Meet Justin

Justin, how old were you when your asthma started?

"I was three."

How did you find out?

"I had an attack and my mom and dad had to bring me to the hospital for a breathing treatment."

Were you scared?

"Yes. I had never been to the hospital. I didn't know what was happening. I had to go for breathing treatments a lot when I was little."

Do you have allergies?

"Yes."

What are you allergic to?

"I know I'm allergic to cats."

Do you know your triggers?

"One thing is exercise. Also, mold and dust."

What do you have to do special?

"When I was little, I couldn't have any stuffed animals in my room. My mom had to wash down the walls of my room every week. I had to have a special pillow. I'm better now. I still have a special pillow. I take my medicine before I go out to play."

Do you play sports?

"Yes, I like to play soccer and I like to swim."

What do you do to take care of yourself?

"Well, I take my medicine and use my peak flow meter every day. I eat good food. I exercise, but I take medicine first. I keep my room clean."

What would you like other kids to know about asthma?

"If you have asthma, take your medicine. It makes you so much better. It is awful when it's hard to breathe."

If exercise causes an asthma flare, use an inhaler before you start.

Glossary

allergies (AL er geez) — an overreaction of the body to harmless things like dust, could involve a skin rash or sneezing

asthma (AZ mah) — a breathing problem

contract (con TRAKT) — to tighten, to shrink

dander (DAN der) — dry flaky skin from dogs or cats

flare (FLAYR) — sudden attack

inhale (in HAIL) — to breathe in

mucus (MYOO cus) — a fluid made by the body

nebulizer (NEB yuh LIE zer) — a machine that turns liquid medicine into mist

treatment (TREET ment) — medical care

trigger (TRIG er) — to set off

wheezing (WEE zing) — making a high whistling sound

Further reading

Gosselin, Kim. *The ABC's of Asthma*. Jay Jo Books, 1998

Ostrow, William. *All About Asthma,* Albert Whitman, 1993

Cater, Siri M. *I'm Tougher Than Asthma*, Albert Whitman, 1996

Visit these Websites

www.aaai.org/public/just4kids/coloringbook

www.med.virginia.edu/medicine/clinical/pediatrics/ chmedctr/tutorials/asthma

31

Index